IMAGES OF ENGLAND

IVYBRIDGE
REVISITED

IMAGES OF ENGLAND

IVYBRIDGE
REVISITED

IVOR MARTIN

TEMPUS

Frontispiece: Civil Defence Corps, Ivybridge, 1944. Some of the people seen here include Mr and Mrs Freemantle, Mr Turner, Mr Word, Esme Pethrick, Sean Pearce, Mollie Fry, Betty Harvey, Bo Hurrell, Lady Marjorie Edwards, Audrey Winton, Violet Bastard, Mrs Booth, Mrs Skidmore, Mr Notte, Mr Walker, Fred Hoare. Betty Harvey ran Harvey's drapers shop and used to collect pots and pans for Ivybridge's Spitfire fund, in 1941.

First published 2005

Tempus Publishing Limited
The Mill, Brimscombe Port,
Stroud, Gloucestershire, GL5 2QG
www.tempus-publishing.com

© Ivor Martin, 2005

The right of Ivor Martin to be identified as the Author
of this work has been asserted in accordance with the
Copyrights, Designs and Patents Act 1988.

British Library Cataloguing in Publication Data.
A catalogue record for this book is available from the British Library.

ISBN 0 7524 3705 4

Typesetting and origination by Tempus Publishing Limited.
Printed in Great Britain.

Contents

	Acknowledgements	6
	Introduction	7
one	Around Ivybridge	9
two	Business and Transport	33
three	The Railway	51
four	Schooling	59
five	The War Years	69
six	Lee Mill Hospital	81
seven	Events and Celebrations	87

Acknowledgements

This book has been made possible with the help and advice from the following people: Alec Roger, Roger Morgan of Carne Frames, Brian Bullock of B&B print, all members of Ivybridge and District Civic Society, Gerald Miles, Stan Rogers, Mike Lewis, and my wife Pauline, for putting up with my mess. Last but not least to Caroline Whetham for her typing skills, and Tempus Publishing, Matilda Pearce in particular, for asking me to do a second volume.

Ivor Martin
June 2005

Introduction

Although human settlement in this area of South Devon goes back thousands of years, as indicated by the remains found on Dartmoor and elsewhere, the main pattern of present-day settlement dates from Saxon times. Cornwood, Fardel, Blachford, Ermington, Harford, Stowford and Ugborough are all Saxon names and listed in the Domesday Book. Ermington may have been first settled around AD 700.

Ivybridge is of much more recent origin. The name 'Ponte Ederoso' is first recorded in 1250 and 'Ivybrugge' in 1292, but these refer to the bridge and not to the village. It seems possible that the rise of Plymouth in the twelfth century would have led to improvements in the roads leading to it and, in particular, to the building of bridges such as the one across the river Erme. Who exactly was responsible for the construction of the first bridge on this site may never be known; four parishes, Harford, Cornwood, Ermington and Ugborough had their boundaries meeting at the bridge and this may indicate a fairly ancient river crossing.

Farms and other enterprises developed in the area over the years and some accounts of Stowford in particular are given in Louise Ryan's book *An Obscure Place* (1973). She records that at the end of the sixteenth century the Manor (as opposed to village) of Ivybridge (or Wodeland) included two farms, three grist mills, an edge mill and a dovecote.

The town of Ivybridge is of eighteenth and nineteenth-century origin, developing in the adjacent corners of the four ancient parishes and not becoming separate from them until the late nineteenth century. Never a truly agricultural village, the turnpike, the paper mills and later the railway seem to have been the main formative influences. Today, the proximity to Plymouth (nine miles) is promoting further growth.

According to Louise Ryan, in 1692, when the Manor of Ivybridge was sold to John Rogers, Merchant of Plymouth, for £1,282 8s 0d there were only two houses and one or two cottages in that part of the present town that lay in Ermington parish and the King's Highway ran along the present line of Blachford Road.

Rogers opened a road along the west bank of the Erme into the village street and built an inn, The Rogers' Arms (sometimes known as the Ivybridge Hotel) on the site of the present Grosvenor House. This was to attract visitors on the Plymouth Eastern turnpike, which had opened in 1758.

Travel at the time was extremely slow and uncomfortable on the poor roads. In 1762 the *Diligence* coach took twelve hours to travel from Plymouth to Exeter at a cost of 15s 0d while Fly Waggons took four-and-a-half days from Exeter to London. Inns became necessary, not merely for the convenience of travellers, but for changing horses on the stage-coach runs.

Ivybridge toll house, on the turnpike at the bottom of Cole Lane, proved relatively profitable compared with any others, £500 a year being collected from the traffic on the road.

Under an act of authorisation, dated 1820, straightening of the road and the construction of a new bridge was brought about sometime before 1826. Greenwood's map of 1827 shows its new course over the Erme but with the road still taking its old course down Fore Street (as it now is), through woodland and Cadleigh to Lee Mill bridge. The new road is the present line of the A38 from Westover to Lee Mill.

By 1844, it was possible to get from Plymouth to Exeter in only three-and-a-half hours by coach and the mail coach *Quicksilver* took only twenty-one-and-a-quarter hours for the whole journey from London to Devonport (in Plymouth).

Other turnpikes in this area recorded by Lyson's *Magna Brittanis* in 1822 are one from Ivybridge (nearer South Brent) to Totnes, and one from Ivybridge via Meavy, Walkhampton and Sampford Spiney to Tavistock. An 1812 Plymouth guide shows a 'New Road Proposed to Ivybridge' running from Bideford Bridge (Bittaford) to Princetown and a later edition of the same map simply 'New Road to Ivybridge'. Such a road was never built, of course, but there is an 'Ivybridge Lane' leading on to the moor between the Devil's Elbow and the Plume of Feathers at Princetown.

In February 1841 the Quicksilver Mail was embedded between Ivybridge and Laira due to heavy snowfalls. Traffic was suspended until a gang of seventy labourers dug out the vehicle. After the letters had been conveyed to Ivybridge on saddled horses, a road was cut through the snow and quite an array of obstructed coaches dispersed for London and Plymouth.

The coming of the railway in the middle of the nineteenth century meant the end of the stage coaches and the demise of the turnpikes; as railways expanded, turnpike trusts were wound up. Ivybridge toll house was sold in 1874 for £116; it was demolished during road widening in 1930. The one at Bittaford remains, somewhat rebuilt, as a private house.

Charles Hankin

The late Charles Hankin
(1906-1997), fellow historian.

one

Around
Ivybridge

Above: The mouth of the river Erme above Harford, near Ivybridge, before it meanders away over rocks, weirs, through fields, villages and towns. The river gave rise to industry by way of power or as a supply of clean water for the mills, which dotted its route in the eighteenth century, and which led to the establishment of the village of Ivybridge.

Left: There are many little pools along the river Erme like the one seen on this postcard, but when she is in full flood, watch out!

Right: Three gentlemen enjoying a trip to Erme Head, start of the river Erme, above Harford.

Below: Harford Bridge over the river Erme. The river starts at Erme Head, above Harford, and meanders down to Ivybridge.

The head on the wall at Homer's Bridge, Harford. A 'face' can just be made out on right-hand side, in the middle of this postcard.

Another view of the river Erme at Harford, before she meanders down to Ivybridge.

Above and below: Lukesland House, Harford. The house was built in the Gothic style in 1862 and replaced the original house known as Lukesland Grove, of which some stonework remains. The first major landscaping of the garden took place in the 1880s by the then owner James McAndrew. Since then more planting and building has taken place, including: an arboretum, bridges and ponds; and in 1982 a new garden was started.

The river Erme running through farmland past the former Bullaven Farm Hotel. The hotel boasted riding, golf and swimming, among other country, pursuits between 1920 and 1930. The tariff was 3½ guineas per person per week or 12/6p to 25/– daily, all in!

A tranquil view if the river Erme at Flete, near Ivybridge.

The river passes through Ermington and Fleet and then on to Wonwell, a popular destination for outings.

The Square, Ermington, which still looks the same today. Every year, on the third Saturday in June, Ermington holds the Bridge Ceremony, when the good folk of Ermington 'block the bridge'. After some dialogue, Ivybridge pays Ermington a toll of one fat duck from the river, a ream of paper from the mill and one red rose. This is accompanied by a 'gate dressing'.

Above: Cornwood Square, *c.* 1900. The view is still the same today, but cars have replaced the horses.

Left: Edmond Pinwell, vicar of St Peter's church, Ermington between 1880 and 1924, was born in Holberton where his father was the vicar. His mother was the daughter of Modbury vicar William Stackhouse.

St Peter's church, Ermington, with its crooked fourteenth-century spire.

This rather large group, dressed in their finery, are seen here enjoying a day out at Mothercombe, *c.* 1900.

Cottages at Bittaford.

The Horse & Groom public house, Bittaford, now on the opposite side of the road.

View from Ivybridge end of the viaduct. The large house at the end of the viaduct is now the Horse & Groom public house.

Cornwood, 1906. Most of the cottages in this photograph are still in existence. Cornwood then boasted a blacksmith and a wheelwright. Dating back from the sixteenth century, the village of Cornwood has prospered on Dartmoor's clay pits. Martin Bros Clayworks discovered a way to make building bricks from the waste at the clay works.

Yeo Cottages, sited on the riverbank, still exist today. According to the 1861 census for Cornwood, Philip Chapple lived at No. 74 Yeo Cottages, James Luscombe at No. 75 and Richard Hillson at No. 76. All men were listed as labourers.

The Cornwood Inn. John H. Glover was the licensee of this old coaching inn in 1901, which offered stabling for horses, as indicated. According to the 1861 census for Cornwood, thirty-two-year-old George Jones was listed as innkeeper of the Cornwood Inn at this time.

Interior of Cornwood parish church in the 1920s. St Michael's is a fifteenth-century church, much restored, with a chancel and west tower dating from around 1300. There is a seventeenth-century pulpit, and there are a few mural monuments to local families. The sender of this postcard wrote to a friend in Plymouth to say they were 'having a lovely time and lovely weather'.

Above and below: The most interesting house in the parish of Cornwood is Fardel, a Saxon estate and a Domesday manor. It came to the Raleigh family by marriage in the fourteenth century and remained in the family until Carew Raleigh, son of Sir Walter Raleigh, sold it. The house is a medieval mansion, with a well-preserved chapel. In 1860, the first stone with an Ogham inscription to be discovered in England was found near Fardel. This stone is now in the British Museum.

Above: Ugborough parish church, St Peter's, lies in a prehistoric earthwork. At the time this photograph was taken, in the early 1900s, the village contained a congregational chapel, a reading room, a board school and a police station.

Right: Ugborough church plate, normally kept in a bank for safe keeping. The Chalice is Elizabethan (Exeter type) retained by the church at the time of the Reformation. The two silver Patans date from the 1720s. The silver flagon dates from 1784 and the Alras dish from 1681.

Two Longhorn cattle from Cotswold Rare Breeds Farm, they appeared in the film *Brave Heart*. Ugborough House is in the background.

The Chantry, an old vicarage in Station Road (behind Victoria Park), *c.* 1900.

The chapel of St Andrew and Gaye Tower, Filham House. Sited in the garden of Filham House, the chapel dates from 1402, and the tower from the eighteenth century. It is rumoured that they were once used by monks, as was the lake, from which they caught their supper!

The town of Ivybridge is an historic settlement situated on the south-west border of Dartmoor National Park. It took its name from the ancient ivy bridge over the river Erme, which dates back to around the early thirteenth century, and used to mark the parish boundaries of Cornwood, Ermington, Hartford and Ugborough. In the eighteenth century Ivybridge was a small but thriving community based around the now-demolished London Hotel, used as a staging point on the road to and from Exeter and Plymouth. The growth of Plymouth brought a great increase in traffic along this road, however, the bridge was only wide enough to take pack horses and riders. The present bridge is a single-arched structure now bypassed by a modern bridge.

Fore Street, Ivybridge, early 1900s. Fore Street (now pedestrianised) and Western Road were once part of the main road from Exeter to Plymouth from the days of the pack horse until the A38 was opened in 1973. When the bypass was opened, access to Plymouth and Exeter became easier and Ivybridge quickly grew into a town in 1977. Glanville's Mill shopping precinct and a new leisure centre was built to meet the needs of the growing population.

Dorothy Cane, who lived at Hunsdon Farm, Ivybridge, was a champion butter maker. At the turn of the twentieth century, most of Ivybridge's population either worked in the mills or on the land. A thriving farmers' market continues in Ivybridge to this day.

An early photograph of the Bowls Club, 1930s.

The bowling green at Gentry Avenue. The Bowls Club still meet at the same venue but now have a new club house.

The first changing hut at the open-air swimming pool in Long Timber Wood, later exchanged with a brick block-built one.

The Dowdell family lived at No. 30 Fore Street, before emigrating to Canada in 1924. From left to right, back: Alfred, Maud, William, Walter. Front: -?-, Grace, Cyril. Alfred and Cyril acquired nicknames at Station Road School: Alf Titbits and Cyril Shoot Doots.

A letter to William Lethbridge of No. 50 Fore Street. This address is now a hairdresser's, next door to an ironmonger. Number 50 Fore Street was not built until after 1890. Before this there were cottages set back from the road and even now, behind the ironmongers, there are the remains of these cottages, one up one down, with just a ladder in one corner to get upstairs. Between the two shops is a tarmac lane, under which are the original cobbles. They were covered up when customers of the garden centre (then at rear) were finding it difficult to keep their footing. This letter was sent overland via France from someone in the Crimean War.

The Spurrel family, 1910.

The interior of St John's parish church, Ivybridge, built and consecrated in 1882. There was a chapel here as early as 1402.

The choir from St John's parish church, 1930s. The only lady identified in this picture is Winnie Stone, third from the left in the front row.

A Victorian family group outside 'Nirvana', Blatchford Road. The house was built by a tea planter when he retired back to England. A book containing sketches and watercolours of Niagara Falls, and places from around Canada, Devon (including Harford near Ivybridge), and Cornwall, were drawn by Ms L. Morris, one of the young ladies from this family in the 1880s, so she was certainly a traveller.

Above: The Bridge Inn, in the early part of century. The adjoining row of cottages remain almost unaltered today. The children are probably on their way to or from Station Road School.

Left: Green Street, now demolished, in the 1940s. The young girl in the photograph is now Mrs Sheila Jewars, who remembers bathing in the old tin bath in front of the fire, and having to use the old outside 'privvy' in the right-hand corner of this photograph.

two

Business and Transport

A blacksmith hard at work making horseshoes in his workshop. Ivybridge once supported three smithies, and today a mobile smithy still services the area.

Left: Mr Baber, saddler of some repute. His shop in Fore Street was where Newsome's optician is now. He kept some very good ledgers – one entry that keeps cropping up is W.A.C. or L.A.C, which stands for 'won at cards' or 'lost at cards', but after his son was born, no more cards!

Opposite above: Stone-breaking at Stowford, looking up Warren Hill. Quarried stone would be carted to the roadside where the stone breaker would reduce the stone to the size required for road repairs. Payment was calculated by the yard of stone broken, and measured by the contractor.

Opposite below: The horse-drawn Ivybridge to Modbury bus climbing Modbury Hill in the late 1800s. The service was run by Mr Steven and operated on Mondays, Wednesdays, Thursdays and Saturdays in 1870.

The toll house at the corner of Cole Lane and Exeter Road, before the new bridge was built in 1826 and the road straightened.

Opposite above: Among the local traders in Ugborough were a grocer, draper, blacksmith, miller, mason, shoemaker and builder, as well as two local inns, the Ship and the Anchor.

Opposite below: Sorting rags at a papermill to be made into postage stamps.

Above: The original Grosvenor House, when it was known as the London Hotel – a popular coaching inn.

Left: The Old Post House and Grosvenor House on Western Road. Grosvenor House, built around 1800, was once a coaching inn called the Rogers' Arms. The first Ivybridge post office was situated in a room in the Old Post House before the Fore Street Post Office building was built in 1909. It was used to billet personnel during the First World War and later became a doctor's surgery, until the Health Centre was built on Station Road in 1969. The building is today a residential home for the elderly.

Above: The premises of C.R. Leigh & Son, tailors and outfitters at No. 9 Erme Road in the early 1920s. The building is currently a betting shop.

Right: A receipt dated January 1922 from C.R. Leigh & Son for a pair of tweed trousers for Mr Cursons, a local builder in Fore Street, costing £2 2s.

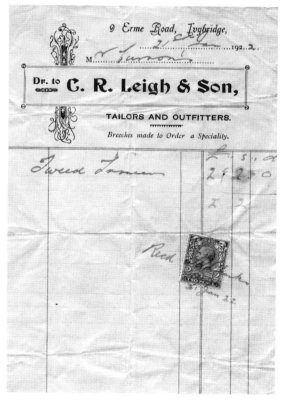

Luscombe & Harris,
Family Butchers

Families waited on daily.

❧

Best Quality Meat Only.

61, FORE STREET,

J. WHIDDON
(Late E. HENLEY).

1, Fore Street, Ivybridge

CENTRAL WHIDDON'S STORES. 41

FAMILY GROCER & PROVISION MERCHANT.

TEA & COFFEE SPECIALIST.

This page: Advertisements for local businesses in Ivybridge: Luscombe & Harris, butcher at No. 61 Fore Street, F.J. Whiddon, grocer at No. 41 Fore Street, now replaced by a supermarket, and W.H. Bowden, motor and cycle agent at No. 23 Western Road.

W. H. BOWDEN,
MOTOR & CYCLE AGENT
SOLE AGENCY for Leading Make Cycles.

Machines Hire.

All Accessories kept in stock.

Repairs done.

Motor Cycles.

ACCUMULATORS CHARGED.
Motor Spirits, Oils and Greases stocked.
MOTOR GARAGE AND PIT.

23, Western Road, IVYBRIDGE.
Telephone 5Y4.

Above: The Smallridge family. In the last two decades of the nineteenth century the Smallridges were prominent Ivybridge residents. Richard Smallridge lived at Yew Tree House in Fore Street. He died in 1910 aged eighty-six. Charles Smallridge was a grocer, draper and wine merchant at No. 54 Fore Street. He was also a keen photographer, and amassed a large collection during his lifetime. He died in 1938 aged seventy-nine. It has not been established which branch of the family appear in this picture.

Right: An advertisement for Charles Smallridge's shop at No. 54 Fore Street.

C. SMALLRIDGE & Co's

DELICIOUS

T 2/- T

FOR QUALITY, STRENGTH & FLAVOUR,
CANNOT BE SURPASSED,

+ TRY + IT ! +

IVYBRIDGE SUPPLY WAREHOUSE
54 FORE STREET,

IVYBRIDGE,

AGENTS FOR W & A. GILBEY'S WINES & SPIRITS
BASS' & IND. COOPES ALES
GUINNESS' STOUT.
ROBINSONS' BRISTOL.

A bill and receipt from M. Thomas Motors Ltd, Plymouth, issued to Mr H. Salter of No. 52 Fore Street, Ivybridge, for the purchase of a new Sunbeam-Talbot Ten Saloon car costing £676 15s 10d in October 1946.

Two advertisements from the June 1958 edition of the *Ivybridge & Harford Parish Magazine* for W.W. Luxton Ltd, ironmonger, and Hoare & Sons Coaches, Ivybridge. The late Fred Hoare, founder of Hoare & Sons Coaches, lived at Longtimber Cottage and owned the coach workshop in Park Street. The company was later acquired by the Kingsbridge firm Tally Ho! Coaches Ltd in 1975. For a while this business ran under joint ownership with vehicles remaining in Hoare's livery but carrying the Tally Ho! fleet name. This situation lasted until 1976 by which time the whole undertaking, including the yard and small office building at Ivybridge, were taken over completely by Tally Ho!

Cecil Downing with one of Hoare's coaches in the 1950s. He was also a postman in Ivybridge for many years.

Right: A receipt for a Mr Salter from J. Turner & Son, haulage contractors on Hunsdon Road, for the hire of a skip.

Below: An advertisement for Dingle's department store at No. 54 Fore Street.

VAT Reg. No. 144 0123 21   **work sheet**   No 10473

H.J. & M.C. TURNER

trading as

J. TURNER & SON

HAULAGE CONTRACTORS & SKIP HIRE
Three Acres, Hunsdon Road, Ivybridge
Telephone Ivybridge 2596

Hired to :-   MR SALTER

1 x 4/6 Wheel Tipper Reg. No.   OYL 463R

On hire at   THE ROUND HOUSE
IVYBRIDGE

Time started   1 SKIP EMPTIED

Time finished   AND RETURNED

Signed by   Date 16-8-83

Disaster striked Fore Street in April 1992 when a massive explosion at a fish and chip shop resulted in a blazing inferno. Luckily no one was injured, although some were taken to hospital suffering from smoke inhalation. Adjoining shops were extensively damaged. It was soon rebuilt with a new name; 'Merry ol' Sole'.

Left: An 1827 directory showing the distance in miles, furlongs and perches from Plymouth to various destinations in Devon.

Opposite above: The burnt-out shell of Lee Mill after a fire, February 1908. Lee Mill had been in existence for many years before Henry Fice Lee took it over in the early 1900s. He ran the mill as Corngriste Mill Coal & Coke and also for a short time generated electricity for the town's lights. The mill was run by waterpower from the river Erme, diverted along a leat in Erme Road and under Fore Street into a large turbine (now in Harford Road car park). Many of the town's older residents remember the mill fondly, as, twice a week a travelling picture show was set up there, with a 6d entry fee.

Opposite below: Harris' of Devon paper mill, owned by Holman Bros. The family are still in the paper-making trade in Kent. The mill became Harris Horticultural Depot and is now a housing estate.

Left: Cecil Holman, who later emigrated to New Zealand. His family ran Lee Mill paper business. The family are still in the paper business but are now based in London.

Below: Fire at Stowford Paper Mill, 5 May 1914. The mill was built here in the 1780s, utilising power from the river Erme. The mill was almost completely ruined, but was rebuilt and soon back in production. Stowford Paper Mill was originally built by William Dunsterville of Plymouth in 1787. In 1849 John Allen acquired the mill, and his family continued to run the mill until 1910.

Above: Another view of the fire at Stowford Paper Mill, Ivybridge, 1914.

Right: J. Herbert Mason was born in Ivybridge on 10 July 1827. His father was a miller and importer of wheat from Russia. In 1840, at the age of fourteen, he and his family emigrated to Canada, sailing from Plymouth on 14 May 1842. The journey took seven weeks. When they got to Canada they built a house and called it Ermeleigh. At fifteen, Herbert took a job as accountant to the Farmers' and Mechanics' Building Society, and rose to become one of the most influential Canadian businessmen of his day.

An advertisement for Lee & Son millers who were flour, corn, seed, manure, coal and coke merchants.

The interior of the paper mill, showing a breaker which breaks down rags into fibres to make paper.

Above: A paper-making machine, early 1900s.

Right: Charlie 'Drummer' Lee collecting his MBE at Buckingham Palace for services to paper-making. His nickname originated during his time in the army, where he was a drummer.

Left: Centre cogs from the water wheel that used to drive Lower Mill, 1987. Only the pit is left now. The wheel was to be renovated but has now become too costly. The water turbine in Harford Road car park is one of only two survivors. An old water turbine, known as The Snail, reflects the town's industrial heritage. It is on display next to the river Erme, whose power was used to drive it.

Below: Mill manager, Mr Tony Traill, is presented with a barometer outside the main office of Stowford Mill. Others present include Mr Freemantle, Mr Northmore, Mr Drummer Leigh MBE, Mr Ward and Mr Chistopher. Stowford Mill was built by William Dunsterville of Plymouth in 1787. Its origins as a paper-making facility date back to the late eighteenth century. This small mill, which used rags until the 1970s, prepares specialty papers for various customers.

three

The Railway

Left: In 1891 the Great Western Railway arrived in Devon. The viaduct was based on a design by Isambard Kingdom Brunel and was seen as an engineering masterpiece. The viaduct spanned the gorge through which the river Erme flows and its highest piers, about 120ft high, are built on rocks in the bed of the river. It was later replaced, but the original stone piers can still be seen behind the present viaduct.

Below: The old Ivybridge station, taken from Plymouth side. Stowford House can be seen in the distance. The last man to lock the station was Tom Pettifer in 1959. The new railway station was built forty years after the old station closed.

Staff at the old Ivybridge station in the late 1800s. Can we still get Nectar tea?

Ivybridge GWR station at the turn of the twentieth century. The advertisements include Sunny Island Tea, Epps' Cocoa and Turner & Phillips' pianos, based in Plymouth.

Ivybridge GWR station, 1921. Three porters are assisting two passengers. The only thing left today are the railings.

Ivybridge GWR station in the snow, during the Second World War. The gentleman with the broom is Tom Pettifer.

GREAT WESTERN RAILWAY.

"CONVERSION OF GAUGE."

This is the last Broad Gauge Train to travel over the line between Penzance and Exeter.

.... } { *Traffic Inspector.*

To the
Station Master

.... Station.

May 20th, 1892.

A certificate issued in 1892 to ensure that no broad-gauge engine or stock was stranded in the West Country when the railway was converted to narrow gauge.

The old broad-gauge railway built by Brunel. Stowford House can be seen in the middle distance.

Left: A plaque commemorating the opening of the new Ivybridge station on 15 July 1994. It was unveiled by Cllr Richard Westlake and Martin Reynolds, Director of Railtrack Great Western.

Below: A souvenir ticket commemorating the opening of the new Ivybridge station on 15 July 1994.

IVYBRIDGE STATION

Souvenir ticket to commemorate the opening of Ivybridge station on Friday 15 July.

Valid on the first train from Ivybridge to Plymouth, returning to Ivybridge the same day.

Plymouth ● ● Ivybridge

440087

REGIONAL RAILWAYS ⚡

A train arrives into Bittaford from the Wrangaton side. The old Brunel pillars can be seen. The old chapel, now a dwelling, can be seen on the left.

A deserted Cornwood station, 8 June 1921.

Left: A luggage label from Ivybridge station.

Below: A hunt rides past Kingsbridge Road Hotel, Wrangaton, which served Kingsbridge Road station on the South Devon line. The station, which once boasted a bookstall, was later renamed after the village but the hotel kept up the old name. The hotel has had a few changes of name but since the Devon Express Way was built it has had a chequered history and its future is presently in doubt.

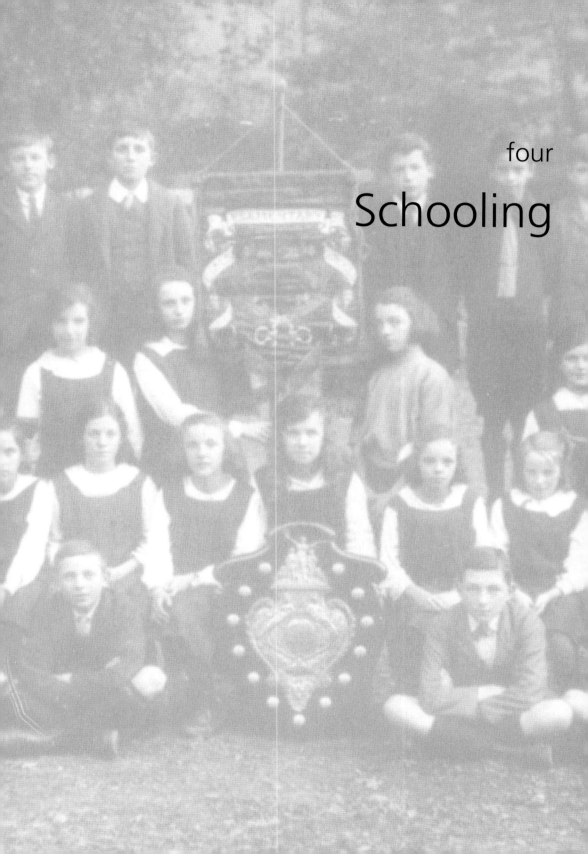

four

Schooling

IVYBRIDGE SCHOOL BOARD.

Russell Buildings.

Plymouth.

4th December 1895.

Gentlemen,

Ivybridge Schools.

At a Meeting of the above Board held on the 2nd instant, the question of the proposed new Lease of the Ivybridge Schools was considered and it was Resolved as follows viz:—

That the Managers be asked if they would be willing to forthwith terminate the present Lease of the Schools and to grant a new Lease of the same to the Ivybridge School Board for a term of 99 9 years at a nominal yearly Rent of Five shillings, subject to the following special conditions viz:—

The Managers to have the exclusive use of the old Schools on all Sundays, and on all weekdays after four o'clock p. m. and of the new Schools on all Sundays, and on one week day after four o'clock p. m. such week day to be a matter of arrangement between the Managers and the Board.

I should be glad therefore if you would kindly consider the above proposals and inform me in due course whether you would be prepared to terminate the present Lease and to grant a new Lease to the Ivybridge School Board on the terms suggested.

Yours faithfully,

John Ashford

Clerk to the School Board.

The Managers of the
    Ivybridge Schools,

Right: An advertisement for the Devon School of Gardening, Ivybridge. The school taught horticulture to ladies and prepared them for the Royal Horticultural Society's exam. The gardens were where Stowford Mill garden is now.

Below: Children from Ivybridge Board School, now The Erme School, playing in Victoria Park. Mr Luxton was the headmaster at Ivybridge Board School in 1927.

Opposite: A letter from the Ivybridge School Board proposing to grant a new lease for a term of 999 years at a nominal yearly rent of 5s.

A class of children from Cornwood Church School, 1911.

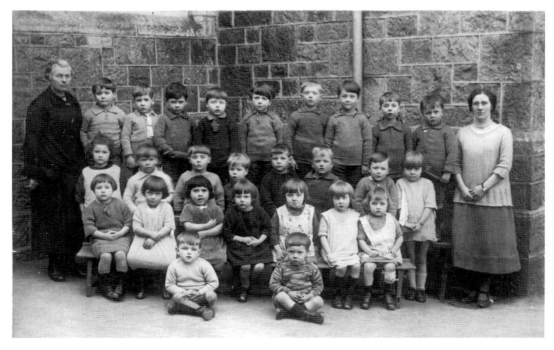

Miss Love and Miss Crose with a class of children from Station Road School, Ivybridge, in the 1920s.

Children from the Erme School, formerly Station Road School. The school was built in 1854 and still exists. It was first extended in 1896 and and again in 2004 to allow for an increase in the number of pupils. The current head teacher is Mr Simon Hall, formerly of Woodland School.

Mr Luxton with the Erme School choir, 1921.

Ivybridge infants' class, 1920s.

Dame Hannah Rogers School, Ivybridge, was originally founded in 1787 for the poor children of Devon and Cornwall. The building reopened in 1949 for the reception of twenty-seven children with Cerebral Palsy, at which time it was only the fourth school of its kind to be opened in the British Isles. The new building was opened by the Queen Mother, is equipped for fifty children and cost £90, 0000.

Youngsters at Ivybridge Community College being introduced to the Second World War with artefacts from the National Ambulance Museum, arranged by Ivybridge and District Civic Society, in conjunction with the National Ambulance Museum.

The Duke of Edinburgh visits Ivybridge Community College, an award-winning sports college situated in Harford Road, in 1982.

Children from the Erme School cutting the first sod for the bypass (Marjorie Kelly Way) with Mayor Joy Day and deputy head Lesley Smith in 1993. The bypass was completed in 1994.

Above: Primary school children enjoy a trip on the first train at the opening of the new railway station in 1994, built with money from the EEC.

Right: Charlotte Lee and Stacy Osborne meet Prime Minister John Major on their first day at school in April 1997. Mr Major was visiting the health centre in the town to see a fund-holding GP practice in action. Despite Devon County Council refusing an invitation for children to meet him, as it was near the election, this was overcome by the PM who shook hands with children over the wall. Devon County Council allowed it, although stipulated that it had not been pre-arranged!

Left: Picture of Erme Primary School, formerly called Station Road School, before the new extension was added in 2004. This section was added in the 1890s. During the Second World War, refugees from London came to Devon, and some of the children attended Station Road School. Mr Lake was the headmaster between 1873 to 1904.

Below: The new Erme Primary School was officially opened by Cllr Brenda Taylor, Vice Chairman of Devon County Council, on 24 June 2005.

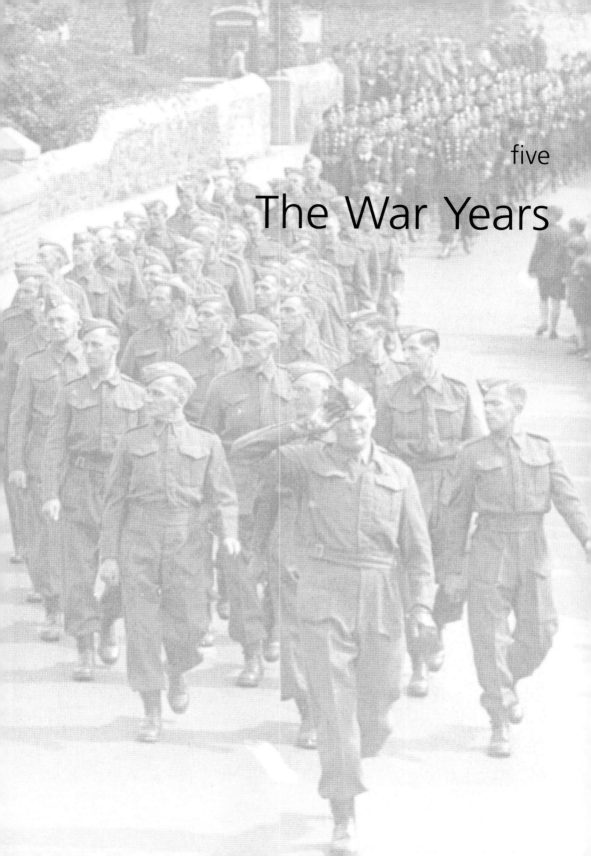

five

The War Years

Above: Building a rifle range at Cleeve. This range was used by the Ivybridge Home Guard to carry out their training.

Left: Reggie Hawker, Captain with the Royal 1st Devon Yeomanry, 1910. He was killed in action in Mesopotamia in 1917. He was uncle to John and Michael Farr.

Opposite above: Camouflage netting team at Station Road School, now Erme Primary School, *c.* 1942. All the ladies seen in this photograph had attended Station Road School until the age of fourteen. They made more nets than anyone else and as a result received a letter from Prime Minister Winston Churchill congratulating them for all their hard work. Among those pictured here are John Talbot, Doreen Vincent and Roy Priddle.

Searchlight personnel at Westlake, mid-1940s. Enemy planes coming in to bomb Plymouth would sometimes approach the city from the east or fly over Ivybridge towards targets in Wales or the Midlands. There were two searchlight batteries operating at Lee Mill and on farmland at Westlake. The Westlake battery was operated by ten men, some sleeping in an old double-decker bus in a nearby field. The searchlight beams would pick up enemy aircraft, and the nearby ack-ack gun unit would go into action when a plane was spotted. Forty personnel made up the compliment of staff who maintained a round-the-clock duty for most of the war.

A group of American GIs relaxing at their camp in Ivybridge, 1944, before leaving to take part in D-Day manoeuvres. Now a housing estate, developers at the time discovered cloth webbing, ammunitions and personal stuff belonging to the GIs.

Leon Freedman on his donkey, at Moorhaven, Bittaford, with American soldiers training behind.

German POWs clearing the entrance to the American camp, 1940s.

PLYMOUTH CITY POLICE

No: *1726*

Date: *2·4·41*

The holder is a representative of _Devon & Cornwall_

Building Soc, 22 Lockyer St. and should be granted facilities to proceed at his own.

risk. This permit should be produced with the holders identity card

Chief Constable

Name: *Elizabeth L. Skidmore,*

Identity Card No:- *W.H.U.W. 277/3.*

A permit and identity card were required for travel during the war years. This permit was issued to Elizabeth L. Skidmore in 1941.

Left: A memorial to the American servicemen from the Bedford 1st Battalion 116th Infantry Regiment stationed at Ivybridge between 1943-44, many of whom never returned from the D-Day invasion on 6 June 1944. Ivybridge has strong ties with Bedford, Virginia, many of whose servicemen were stationed in the town during the Second World War. The memorial was unveiled in Harford Road by Mrs Vera Luscombe, former landlady of the Sportsman public house where American officers drank during their stay in the town.

Below: Ivor Martin and Pat Shepard join in the celebrations at the dedication of the American war memorial. Pat used to deliver milk to American servicemen during the Second World War

ANTI-GAS

I. Personal Decontamination.
C.O.E.C.D.O.

1. *Immediate action*—can be done on the move.

    Cotton waste—Remove free liquid on exposed skin.

    Ointment—Rub vigorously into exposed skin for at least ½ minute—using both hands.

    Eyeshields—If contaminated, remove and renew.

2. If possible to be done under cover or on " clean " ground.

    Clothing—(Not necessary for a few *small* drops).
    Swab off free liquid on cape.
    Remove or cut away contaminated clothing.
    Rub ointment into skin beneath these parts.

    Detectors—Change individual detectors if required.
    Decontaminate weapons.

    Ointment—Wipe hands with *clean* swab.
    Rub ointment into hands for ½ minute.

Notes.—1. *Don't* put your rifle and equipment down on contaminated ground.

2. Swab free liquid off web equipment—apply ointment to both sides where contaminated. You can then wear it again.

Above and below: An information leaflet informing people how to deal with the affects of a gas attack.

II. Gas Alarm System

For United Kingdom and other places where syren cannot be used :—

1. **ONE ALARM**—Gas rattle.
   ONE WARNING—" Spray "—by word of mouth.

2. **RATTLE**—means Gas—other than air spray.
   Action. **HOLD BREATH.**
   Adjust facepiece.
   If *blister* gas—contaminated men also carry out personal decontamination (see over) at first opportunity.

3. **" GAS CLEAR "**
   Action. **TEST FOR GAS.**
   Remove facepiece.

4. **" SPRAY " WARNING**
   Action. Personal decontamination as required (see over).

5. **SENTRIES**—Provided with gas rattle.
   Must know location of spray detectors.

The camp at Lee Mill for displaced families from Plymouth, which suffered some of the worst bombing in the UK during the Second World War.

Lee Mill camp. This was a completely self-contained village and was built on the site where Tesco supermarket and the industrial estate is now.

Churchill's secret army, Ivybridge. These men were expected to go underground if an invasion took place and wait three weeks before re-emerging as saboteurs. Now their bunkers are being sold.

A victory tea held for residents of Hunsdon and Woodland Roads, Ivybridge, 1945.

Above and below: Ivybridge town band and army corps march up Fore Street during VE Day celebrations in Ivybridge, 1945.

Above: The leader of the armed forces at the War Memorial in Ivybridge for the Thank the Soldier procession, 1945.

Below: American soldiers march across the new bridge for the Thank the Soldier procession, 1945.

This poem, sung to the Widdecombe Fair tune, was written about men from the Ugborough Home Guard during the Second World War. Some of the men mentioned are still alive today.

This is the tale of our Home Guard,
All along down along by the Old Moors,
The men who would fight the Hun had he come,
Wi' Pengelly, Harold Pearse, Jim Pearson, Jim Warner, Arthur Beable,
Tom Spry, Old Private Bill Martin and all, Old Private Bill Martin and all.

At first we were called the L.D.V.
All along down along by the Old Moors,
To fight for England and kept it free,
W' Len Beable, Fred Kevern, Jack Carroll, Ken Watts, Bob Blank,
Donald Welch, Old Uncle Bert Beer and all, Old Uncle Bert Beer and all.

With shot guns, pop guns, sticks and stones,
All along down along by the Old Moors,
Watching out day and night away from our homes,
Wi' Jack Handford, Tubby Watts, Harry Jane, Charlie Marsh, Charlie Derrett,
Ben Bennett, Old Charlie de Cerjat and all, Old Charlie de Cerjat ND all.

Soon they dressed us in khaki and gave us all guns,
All along down along by the Old Moors,
We had to slope arms and march with the things,
Wi' Roy Andrews, John Thomas, Jack Pinhey, Fred Willcocks, John Hodge,
Tom Lloyd, Young Henry Pinhey and all, Young Henry Pinhey and all.

We worked hard for our livings all the long day,
All along down along by the Old Moors,
We trained evening and Sundays without getting pay,
I' Fern Hines, Tom Woodley, George Bartlett, Bill Bartlett, Jack Hines,
Fred Tucker, Old Ivor Davies and all, Old Ivor Davies and all.

We went on manoeuvres in sun and in rain,
All along down along by the Old Moors,
(One called Darke was damned cold but Sopers Stew was just hot,
The price of that night out we've never forgot),
Wi' Roy Andrews, Ern Sampson, Ray Harvey, Ray Cole, Harry Crocker,
Tubby Anstice, Old sgt Hurrell and all, Old sgt Hurrell and all.

Bert Fox's old lorry was the transport for us,
All along down along by the Old Moors,
Then headquarters provided us with a bus,
For Jack Hil, Bill Luscombe, Arthur Billing, Dick Anstice, Bert Terry, Hubert Rowe,
Old George Smale and all, Old George Smale and all.

Our wives were all lonely and our girls all sad,
All along down along by the Old Moors,
But could they have seen us they might have been nad,
At our shooting, wood clearing, right turning, house clearing,
Left turning, field training, the Old P.S.I. and all, the Old P.S.I. and all.

six

Lee Mill
Hospital

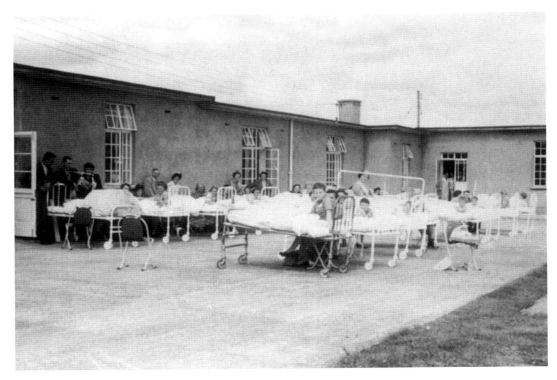

Patients from the children's ward at Lee Mill Hospital. The hospital opened in 1934. It took over from a hospital ship called *Maine* that the Health Authorities had moored in Plymouth Sound to take infectious cases like smallpox. The boat was rusting away and needed to be replaced by accommodation in a rural area, so they purchased the land from the Abbots family, local farmers.

The original wooden huts were used for workmen building Burrator Reservoir before being moved in 1939 to Lee Mill to form the hospital building. Some of the wooden huts remained until they were demolished when the hospital became a Primary Care Trust Secure Unit in 1989.

Lee Mill Hospital II. Stan Rogers who worked at the hospital with his wife, both of whom contracted smallpox, the unfortunate Mrs Rogers three times. It was converted into a reserve maternity unit for Freedom Fields Hospital in Plymouth, in case of bombing during the Second World War, but was never used for this after all. It then became a children's hospital for polio victims and other various ailments.

The hospital later became an elderly person's hospital until it closed, despite much opposition, in July 1989. In a last defiant effort the staff built a float for the Ivybridge Carnival showing a sinking ship. A new building was erected, which became a Primary Care Trust Unit, and is now mainly used to accommodate people with mental health problems.

Opposite above: The Royal Marine from HMS *Drake* band entertain children in West Ward at Lee Mill Hospital, 1955.

Opposite below: Children play in the snow – all part of the treatment at Lee Mill Hospital, 1945.

A sunny day trip to Mount Wise, Plymouth, for children from Lee Mill Hospital, helped by their Navy friends, *c.* 1940.

Above and opposite page: Children from Lee Mill Hospital enjoying a day out to Mount Batten, Plymouth, accompanied by naval friends, *c.* 1940.

Len Jackman, organist extraordinaire, with a small group of nurses and patients, sadly almost at the end of the hospital's life.

seven

Events and Celebrations

Above: A horse-drawn float decorated for the coronation of King George VI, 1937. Stowford House is in the background.

Left: In 1580, explorer and naval captain Francis Drake completed the first circumnavigation of the world by an Englishman, for which he was knighted aboard the *Golden Hind* by Queen Elizabeth I. This is depicted in part of the stained-glass window in Stowford House which was installed in the mid-nineteenth century. The 400th anniversary was celebrated at Stowford Mill by a specially produced watermarked paper depicting Drake with his ship, the *Golden Hind*.

Opposite above: Town officials and local dignitaries attend the opening of the Butterbrook Reservoir in June 1916, which cost £17,000 to build.

Elephants from Fosset's Circus stop for a drink from the leat outside Lee & Sons' mill, 1950. They arrived by train and then walked up to Woodlands where the circus was set up and locals treated to a show in the big top. One year, they even went to Lee Mill Hospital to entertain the children and patients, with a clown, stilt-walker and elephants.

A 'Gay Nineties' Christmas party, 9 January 1947.

Cavemen from the historical pageant, 1950.

Carnival time, August bank holiday, 1944. Barbara House is dressed as Lottie the horse, and Gladys Richards as the clown.

Opposite: Historical pageant, 1950. Barbara House and Pat Withycombe are among the group.

PROGRAMME 2D.

* * *

"The Marriage of Father Time"

A MUSICAL FARCE

Written and Produced
by

J. GORDON BROWN

A programme for *The Marriage of Father Time* at Lee Mill Estate.

1st Ivybridge Wolf Cubs, 1923. From left to right, back row: Mrs Roberts and Mrs Patey. Middle row: T. Turner, J. Gard, A. Northmore, E. Bowden, P. Maddock, G. Brownstone, G. Hattrick. Front row: E. Maddock, W. Lake, I. Williams, C. Varcoe, H. Bryant, C. Pippin, ? Williams, L. Hattrick.

1st Ivybridge Company. Boys' and Girls' Brigades, June 1996.

Right: Tina and Lesley with their entry for the 'Guy' competition, November 1980.

Below, middle: Every year, on the third Saturday in June, Ermington holds the Bridge Ceremony, when the good folk of Ermington 'block the bridge'. After some dialogue, Ivybridge pays Ermington a toll of one fat duck from the river, a ream of paper from the mill and one red rose. This is accompanied by a 'gate dressing'. The town mayor is seen here exchanging gifts with local schoolchildren.

Michelin Man (Sid Ingram) in the office of the mill where some paper was being made for the tyre manufactures. Present are Gwen, Rolly, Mo, Jim, Miss Jewel and Courtney Pippin.

Above: Santa arrives in Ivybridge to switch on the Christmas lights in Fore Street, helped by two shire horses from Yealmpton. Brian Scown, Mayor of the town, is Santa.

Left: A painting by Marianne Kirks, commissioned for the Mayor to auction at a civic fund-raising dinner.

Opposite above: A rally was organised in the grounds of Lord Clifford's home, Ugbrook House, depicting 'past times', in order to raise funds for the Devon Air Ambulance. Some of the items featured were these Victorian bath chairs and Penny Farthing bicycles.

Opposite below: Ivor Martin presents the keys to the new community bus to John the driver at County Hall, home of Devon County Council, with Sally Jenkins the co-ordinator, in 2001.

Other local titles published by Tempus

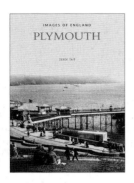

Plymouth

DEREK TAIT

Plymouth has seen many changes over the years and this collection of over 200 archive photographs and postcards features many images of a pre-war Plymouth now long gone. There are nostalgic glimpses of the old pier, Plymouth Hoe and the grand old theatres, where Harry Houdini and Laurel and Hardy were among the performers. This book is sure to bring back memories for all who know and love this city.

0 7524 3128 5

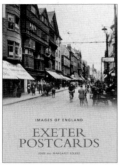

Exeter Postcards

JOHN AND MARGARET FOLKES

This is an exploration of Exeter and Exonians, in the dramatic first six decades of the twentieth century, seen through over 200 archive postcards. Subjects examined include momentous events such as the arrival of the first aeroplanes ever seen by Exonians and the many crises of accidents, fires, floods and war. *Exeter Postcards* provides a fascinating visual history of the city, which will surprise some and reawaken memories for others.

0 7524 3474 8

Dartmoor

TOM GREEVES

The rich history of Dartmoor can be seen in the 200 archive photographs and postcards in this book. The images recall life as it once was on Dartmoor: the towns, villages and local people who lived and worked on the moor between the 1860s and the 1950s. From farming and mining to social gatherings such as hunts, races and fairs, each picture records the everyday life of these resilient communities.

0 7524 3146 3

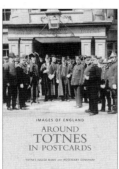

Around Totnes in Postcards

TOTNES IMAGE BANK AND ROSEMARY DENSHAM

This selection of 180 postcards from the Totnes Image Bank collection illustrates the history of this town and the surrounding area, including Dartington, Ipplepen and Ashprington. The ancient castle and Elizabethan buildings are featured and events such as carnivals, Empire Day celebrations and the relocation of the Victoria Memorial Fountain are recalled.

0 7524 3190 0

If you are interested in purchasing other books published by Tempus, or in case you have difficulty finding any Tempus books in your local bookshop, you can also place orders directly through our website

www.tempus-publishing.com